SEED

Seed

David Eye

THE HILARY THAM CAPITAL COLLECTION
2017 Selections by Eduardo C. Corral

THE WORD WORKS
WASHINGTON, D.C.

ISBN: 978-1-944585-14-3
LCCN: 2016957978

Acknowledgments

Many thanks to the editors of the journals and anthologies where these poems first appeared, some in different forms or with different titles:

Between: New Gay Poetry (Chelsea Station Editions): "Unspoken at JFK" (reprint)
Bloom: "Video Booth Sonnet"
Chelsea Station: "Protocol" and "Bass and Guitar"
Cider Press Review: "As New York Snow" and "Say You're Walking on a Beach"
Consequence Magazine: "Unspoken at JFK"
Critical Encounters with Texts (Pearson): "Negative (1996)"
The Good Men Project: "Targets" (reprint) and "Unspoken at JFK" (reprint)
Lambda Literary: "Dance Bar" and "Leavings"
The Louisville Review: "Crossing," "The Stream Empties into a Field," and "Targets"
Mayday Magazine: "Across the Galaxy"
Motif 3: All the Livelong Day, an Anthology of Writings about Work (Motes Books): "Ecstasy"
Puerto del Sol: "MTA I: 3rd Ave Bus"
roger: "MTA III: Woman with OCD"
Rondeau Roundup: "A Distant Line of Hills"
The Queer South: Essays and Poems (Sibling Rivalry Press): "Pond"
Stone Canoe: "All I Have," "Last Day, Land's End," "Morning, Delft Haven," "Photo: Fort Sam Houston, 1984"
Touching: Fearless Poetry Series Vol. 2 (Fearless Books): "A Blond Woman"
Waccamaw: "Not That You Asked"

I am grateful—

—to my teachers. To Robin Becker, who started it all at the Fine Arts Work Center; for the generous scrutiny of Michael Burkard, Brooks Haxton, Mary Karr, Chris Kennedy, and Bruce Smith at Syracuse University; for Marie Ponsot's gentle urging at The New School; and for Charles Martin's and A.E. Stallings's subtle shaping at Sewanee. A special thank you to Christina Stoddard for her keen eye, and to Bruce Smith for a final once-over. And I am deeply indebted to the late Claudia Emerson for her encouragement before, during, and after my graduate studies.

—to Ron Mohring for publishing my chapbook, *Rain Leaping Up When a Cab Goes Past*, in the Editor's Series at Seven Kitchens Press, 2013.

—for the support of the Sewanee Writers' Conference and the West Chester University Poetry Conference.

—to Eduardo C. Corral, for bringing this manuscript into the light of day, and to Nina Budabin McQuown and Nancy White, for helping me make it a book.

—that my dad is no longer recognizable as the father figure in these poems.

Contents

Three

for my mother

Frontispiece, *Picea excelsa*

This is a tree—a painting of a tree. A copy
of a painting of a Norway spruce in a book,
copyright 1926, seven years older than my father.

His name inside the dark green cover. The book
is made of trees. The leaves have yellowed.
Spruce leaves are needles, evergreen. I can't imagine

my father ever took an interest in trees. His father
was a forester; we share a middle name. I took
the book from his shelf in the house where my father

grew up, which may have been different had his father
not died when my father was fifteen. And maybe then,
when I was fifteen, I wouldn't have wanted my father

to die like his. Fifteen years ago, I planted
seven Norway spruces by the road in front
of my house to shield it from winter's hard stare.

One

Not That You Asked

All the farm boys with tractors in their veins,
and I couldn't back a wagon worth a damn.
Jackknife after jackknife. But horticulture—
field study, color plates, Latin names in viny script—
I knew my way around. Loblolly and scrub pine,
classed by needles per cluster, shape of cone.
The sweet, sharp scent of sun on dry needles,
I run this rugged Catskill trail, negotiating
roots and rock, and my mind trips back
into the Carolina pines where you said
"Even the creek has an Om. Listen."
If you were here I'd still run alone,
your ballet muscles native to the stage.
Around my house, white ash, shagbark
hickory, sugar maples with their easy roots,
and a lone white pine. Wildflowers this time
of year are mostly goldenrod, New York aster.
One blazes in noonday meadows. The other
glows after sundown in the darkening wild
edges of the yard, small clouds of palest blue.

Letter from the Catskills

Cousin—When a dozen robins blew into the yard yesterday—
I'd never seen so many—I watched them hop, cock their heads,
grab the thaw's first worms. Such a pleasure, those yam-
colored breast feathers. Then snow last night, enough
for a fine white pelt, mostly gone by midday. (You're better
off doing your play in the City, till it warms up for good.)
I wonder if the snow melted or—what's that word?—
sublimed. To go from solid to gas, skipping liquid altogether.
The way I'd like to die. Grocery-shopping last night, I swear
I felt like such a loser. Not a full set of teeth in the house,
yet *I'm* the freak: 45, alone at the Liberty Shop-Rite. And a snob:
can you believe it took four people to help me find capers?
So many breakups. My sister got the only keeper. God, I love
those kids. I dream of children almost every night. Awake,
I'm a eunuch. New vocal warmup, repeat before you go on
tonight: "unique New York eunuch unique New York
eunuch . . . ." Give your boy a squeeze. The robins are back.

Dance Bar

Seven of us stranded on the tipsy floor.
The tall Pole wants me to take him home

but other lips are more insistent—Christine—
and he leaves me to her. We can't stop kissing.

Her mouth softer than a man's but with an ardor
in a sheath of softness. Like a hardon. I feel her up

say You know I'm— She'd thought maybe, then
comes against the heel of my hand. On the sidewalk

she says much as I like kissing I want you to fuck me.
I say Much as I like kissing I can't fuck you. Fuck you

she says. In her green eyes, in her face gone slack:
What am I doing and *Who is this guy* and *Faggot*.

Four a.m. streets empty but for hissing taxis,
drizzle-slicked to a high gloss, streaks of stoplight

makeup bleeding red and green and Christine halting
toward 6th Avenue. I catch up, Can I put you in a cab?

No answer but tears.
I walk a block and when I look back

she's following. She hasn't moved. This
City. This: rain leaping up when a cab goes past.

MTA I: 3rd Ave Bus

A gray-haired woman just inside the door
offers a tract and a smile. I decline
the former, return the latter, and take
a window seat. Tree branches usher us
uptown. Two or three stops later a blond
woman in her thirties I think accepts
the woman's leaflet and sits beside me:
"What Must I Do to Be Saved?" She reads it
front to back, then slides it into her bag,
extracting a thick paperback, bookmark
wedged in the chapter "Anal Specialties"
in *Leathermen's Guide to the Universe*
and the old woman presses another
pamphlet into a rider's open hand.

Basement

Back in the cinderblock corner
  beside the iron bed
the big man has cocked his arm
  and smacked the boy's face.

Head down, his nose drips
  onto the bedspread
he'd outgrown, dotting red
  the pale blue sea,

a ship's wheel, twisted rope.
  He doesn't move or wipe,
lets his nose leak *Look
  what you did.* This burning

vessel. How to navigate.
  When the boy lifts
his head, it's not the trail of blood
  across the lip (half

a red mustache) and past the chin
  that strikes the man, but rather
the eyes *You hit me again, I swear—*
  Each studies the other.

In the steady gaze the man
  sees a boy slapped
into manhood and doesn't
  touch him again.

Protocol

for Hart Crane

The comfort of a seaside town
Is that water always edges land.
Cobbles give way to boardwalk,
A few more steps to sand. Twice
A day the tide swells to the seawall,
Now withdrawn beyond the dock:
Fertile ground for night maneuvers.
A tiny flash, then the glowing eye
Of a cigarette. Pulse in your ears,
The moon between slats throws
Brilliant stripes on creosote pilings,
Barnacled joists. You negotiate
The giving sand, climb crisscross
Planks toward men rutting in shadow.
Gentlemen and sailors stand and wait.
You know the code, the protocol.
Feet apart, the young man's hip-jut
Stance invites: you reach for the first
Of thirteen buttons on his pants.
An anxious wave sighs and hisses,
The smell and taste of the sea.
A final surge, gradual ebb.
The pockmarked moon leaves pale
Ribbons on freshly furrowed sand.

Photo: Fort Sam Houston, 1984

Buzz-cut lieutenant, snappy salute, straight-
wrist envy of his troops, confident stride,
inspection-ready platoon, he's checking
haircut and bootshine—In the battalion

up the hill, Nurse Corps officers under
suspicion, hemorrhaging names—Each medic
barracks (Alpha, Bravo, Charlie, Delta)
hunkers like a giant cockroach, spilling

tender, teeming nymphs into the shadow
of its high underbelly—His name drops
into the witch-hunt cauldron—From afar
they're indistinguishable. Closer now,

the investigation: Army lawyer
grills his boss (captain, female, in the know)
about the company he keeps. She throws
a curve, risking her name with what is not.

One Friday, walking to his car, a fist
in his throat from another week's tampdown,
he hasn't quite reached the parking lot when
he is ambushed by a volley of tears.

All I Have

for John

The day I said I was leaving we stayed that way
all afternoon: poles of a magnet.

I could hear him: his silence. Dust motes swarmed
in the window. Twin trapezoids

of light slid across the floorboards, merged, crawled
up the wall, fading. I stood and pushed

through the heavy air of our apartment, the waning
light. Leaning in the bedroom doorway.

He sat cross-legged on the bed, the balled tissues
around him a flock of sleeping doves.

Dusk smearing the room gray. *I'm sorry*—the best I could do.
I wish he had spit or hit me or yelled.

Instead: *I have less than fifty T-cells.*
HIV, I knew. But fifty meant AIDS: "full blown." *All I've got left.*

He must have known when, months before, he asked me
to help him die, take his life if it came to that.

We were walking home from dinner and I hadn't answered
then. *Now*, I thought, *I won't have to.*

MTA II: Downtown F

An old Chinese man
plays a Chinese violin.
Bamboo, snake skin, horse
hair make a sound more
than 1500 years old.

His sign reads:
        Erhu
        Peculiarity: two strings
        A on the outside
        D on the inside

There's no escape for the bow
once set between strings,
prisoner of A and D
forever destined to sing
haunting Chinese sounds
some 1500 years old—
even though the Chinese man
is sitting at 14th Street
and playing "Oh, Susanna"
with his erhu on his knee.

Snake Hunting

The summer I'd turn eighteen, on the dirt road
below The Knob, I said to my father "No.
I won't do it anymore. I won't help kill
them, or cut off their rattles. You go on,
I'll see you back at the house." My father
got this look if you crossed him, wild-eyed.
It would make your skin crawl because
you knew the coil and strike behind it. But
there by Smith Crick, when he saw I wasn't
budging, he backed down and walked on—
but not up the hill. The last time, summer before,
he'd shot a small one, maybe two feet, near
the rock-face cliff edge where pines
and cedars reach out of the stone all gnarled
from wind like an old man's hands. It had slid
under a rock, all but a few dead inches,
but tough. I had to saw the rattles off, only
five or six plus the button. I pocketed the rattle
and went to wipe off the blade, and the blood—
that rattlesnake blood—was red, red as mine.
'Deed it was. 'Deed and double it was.

The Creek Empties into a Field

She is tugged awake in a strange bedroom.
Takes her a minute—house of her in-laws,
hills of West Virginia. Moonlight slices
a swath across the bed, her husband sleeps.
Cool slates underfoot. She's pulled the light on
in the outhouse, removed the wooden lid
centered over the running water, lifts
her cotton gown. In the glare of the bare
bulb, beneath old calendar photos—chicks,
kittens—she cramps again. Another tug:
the unmooring. Her hands fly down to stem
the slough, fingers slick, amber, red. Liquid
sack falling, fallen, spirited away
by the swift stream, dispassionate midwife.

Photo: August 14, 1968

The kitchen in black & white, birthday at the farm. I know I'm eight from how many candy candle-holders on the chocolate cake my aunt's about to slice. She's fifteen, twelve years younger than my mom. We'd fight and she'd get the blame. My pretty mother directs, her hair in a bouffant high as her smile is wide, and the same shiny-apple cheeks as my grandmother. Grandma has the broadest grin and the box of Neapolitan ice cream, flavors reduced in the photo to light, medium, dark. My sister, nearly four, faces the camera but her arm, like the knife, aims at the cake. She is unsmiling, picture-taking a postponement. I'm slight in the corner by the fridge, big front teeth barely showing, standing close beside my sister, arm on the back of her chair. My face is a miniature of my mother's, the nose, the brows the same. Hardly noticeable at the lower left edge, my grandfather in profile, his arm dark against the thin plastic tablecloth printed with balloons and ribbons, confetti. He would have washed up from working the fields and put on his white shirt for dinner but wouldn't have had much to say. Seven spoons, a stack of saucers. You can just make out the pile of spent candles. Not pictured: my father, behind the State Police camera, accordion front and big round flash like a movie reporter's. I never knew what to expect when I looked his direction, but it was safe enough with a camera between us. I looked nothing like him.

Postcard to My Sister

I awoke to rain from a dream of our house on Morton Lane.
We were kids, and alone, the way we liked. But awake, me
on 24th Street, you on Valley View—with husband, kids—well.
At my worst, you know I still get jealous they came between us?
Otherwise, I merely envy the laughing bedtimes, the Band-Aid
knees. Today I'm at my worst: another night ended as your day
began, 5 a.m. Another day I need what's in your house
in my apartment, this second-floor studio over the schoolyard
where I listen to the deaf kids play on days when it doesn't rain.

This Not This

Belongings pulled into the front room,
with Post-it notes I labeled what would go

with me and what would not. All night
I packed and tagged: couch, books, tapes.

In the trunk, decorations unused this year.
Three silver ornaments (anniversary gifts): *This*.

The furry red and white stocking, your name
on the cuff in Elmer's and silver glitter: *Not this*.

At sunrise I showered. The movers said
Why aren't you taking everything? Breakup

I said, and they hauled everything not labeled
not this down one flight to the yawning truck.

I wanted to be out when you got back, ran
around the room yanking yellow tags off

the things that would stay. Only one I had to leave,
one *not this* I couldn't peel off if I tried.

Fish Tank

Glass panels in a wide chrome frame, elements in place: heater, filter, and pump included on my twelfth birthday, gift from my young aunt. Biking across town to the fish lady, her living room converted to darkness and hum and so much color it hurt. One pound of stone in a brown paper bag, one plastic plant at a time, paid for by pushing brooms at the drugstore. Now three plants, weighted in a layer of green chips and bigger blue pebbles. Months before, in summer, the tank on the picnic table to check for leaks, ten gallons of sunlight, refracting in a hundred directions. I played the piano, liked to read. Beside the tank on my dresser, a booklet, favorites circled: neon tetras, black mollies, Siamese fighters. The males, blood-red or blue-violet, fins like flowing gowns, will fight each other to the death, eat their own offspring if not kept apart. I made straight A's but failed at Little League—football *and* baseball. All set, but for water and fishes. Which is the day my father, filling the doorway, said *You can't* said *You can't set it up* said *Aquariums are silly* and with something like a smile turned and left the room. My mother, in his wake, didn't say *Where were you when he bought the plants, the stones?* didn't say *Are you going to pay him for those?* didn't say *Not this time. Fill it up. Get the fish. I'll pay.*

Video Booth Sonnet

A plywood wall; below my waist, a hole.
(Good selections—soon I'm in my glory.)
Your fingers tell me what I need to know:
the index on the rim, and on the fourth,
an aphrodisiac. Your wedding ring
reflects the livid screen. I acquiesce,
a primed and willing party to your sin.
I'm not the married one. But I confess
I picture her, and you, and are there kids
and what if no one ever calls me dad.
Give it to me: words I've yet to resist.
We both get what we're after.
Before you leave the stall I hear you spit.
I stick a dollar in: I need a minute.

Odalisque '76

on viewing an untitled b&w photo from
Toby Old's "Standard Deviation Series"

A Black woman with long glazed legs faces
away from dazed Whiteboy gazes, her 'fro
the only softness in the room. A corpse
under study by med students, but for
their beers and shit-eating leers, and her stack
of cash. Another bill on the platform,
ashtrays spilling butts by her ass. Diamonds
long faded in the runway's fusty rug,
flecked and dusty as the owner's toupee.
One leg *en l'air*——g-string fine as hairnets
on the lunchroom ladies who laid on her
an extra roll in eighth grade when she made
straight A's——she is imagining her tub
and how soon can she scrub off all these eyes.

Targets

A dead man in the basement
taped to the cinderblock wall
between two punching bags.
White lines on a black silhouette
like a map of the night sky.
Punctures in tight constellations:
House of Wound. Debilitate.
House of Shoot-to-Kill. You
taught me well. Every year
another caliber: .22, .38, .45.
In the field, yellowed papers
stapled to a box, rocks inside
for ballast. Concentric circles
in a big black dot: Bullseye.
Bullseye. I'm 45 and you aim
at me for no worse crime
than an attempt at betterment.
Letters fired off in your slanted
hand revile but even as you write,
three fingers are trained backward:
You with other women in your sights.
You banging the neighbor. You
finding my mother, Colt .45
in hand, about to make of herself
a target. Because you have never
seen me, you miss your mark.
But I see you. And I remember
how to inhale, hold, squeeze
the trigger on the out-breath.
And the tang of gunpowder
in the waft of gray-blue smoke.

The Aged Director Responds

Age is irrelevant. Always has been.
You may look like rabbits at the start,
but all it takes is "Please" with Southern boys,
bred to serve your elders. ——Predator?
My dear, I found you in the stacks, pawing
through every back issue of *After Dark*.
You were *waiting* for someone like me.
And I distinctly recall saying "May I?"
before I squeezed you through your cutoffs.
You were ready. No one made you follow
to the restroom. I merely placed your hand
where it wanted to go. Your trembling fingers
knew what to do, with some encouragement.
So diligent at your task you wouldn't look
at me. I was quick, but you didn't finish,
as I recall. And *we* weren't finished, were we?
The world is small, these counties even smaller.
Summer next, you were the boy I'd cast unseen!
You gave me such a face when you walked in,
like you thought I'd share our little secret.
And smaller still—now, with face and name,
I knew you'd gone to grade school with our daughter.
I brought a tape from home: both of you singing
soprano in choir. ——Took advantage? Dear,
I offered you the comforts of our home,
saved you from driving back so late after
the technical rehearsal. True, I didn't
mention to your parents or to you
that the wife and kids were out of town.
It must have slipped my mind. But I recall
I showed you to the study, and pulled out
the sofa bed. Even pointed to my
briefcase full of skin mags before retiring.

Sure enough, soon the latches snapped.
You should have seen your cat-and-canary face
when you saw me in the doorway. In your
underpants, aroused, it was only
fitting I invite you to my room.
Granted, "Come with me" is not a question,
but neither was your silence a reply.
You followed like a lamb and we had barely
reached the bed when you—so eager!—took to
suckling like a newborn. The lights were on,
the better to see your face against my belly.
Adamant as you were unskilled, the end
came soon. You gagged but tried hard not to show it.
I could have warned you, I suppose. At least
I thanked you. You excused yourself and closed
the door behind you. I heard the water run,
drifted off, and slept that night like a child.

Leavings

December rain kicking up on itself
from the New York Public Library steps.
At the top, under cover, a paper
shopping bag between us: radio, shirt,
a book or two. I couldn't wrest my eyes
from its brown, or think of anything else.
Not Provincetown a year before, cheating
February, the fevered makeup. Not
separate summer, or the chilly evening
we left at intermission for pasta
and the end at Ralph's on 9th Avenue.
In this mute epilogue, neither of us
wants to leave or be left. Until he shifts
and I grab the bag, take the stairs on a diagonal
and two at a time past the stoic lions, all I am not,
their faces awash in the unequivocal rain.

MTA III: Crosstown Bus

Almost unhinged but not quite,
creased paper drapes like lace on her lap.
There must have been words once,

now mostly inky blotches. She scribbles,
scratches on the fragile letter. Again. Again.
Almost unhinged but not quite,

the compact mirror in her fleshy hand.
She checks, rechecks, sees what I can't, what
there must have been. Words once

made promises they wouldn't keep.
She opens a worn wallet,
almost unhinged but not quite,

counts, re-counts her cash—one bill—
seems about to speak.
There must have been words, once

the money was gone. And hope. And time.
And now this . . . this what? this coming
there must have been words once
almost unhinged, but not quite.

Breakup Poem

If dawn hadn't been so frigid I'd shrunk
into my coat, curled like a question mark,
eyes on the sidewalk, I might not have seen
the canvas bag at the curb. Didn't I

have a city to leave. A train to take
someplace warm and kind. Why did I unzip
the duffel—stuffed with frozen pups, eyes wide
but the eyeballs shrunken in their sockets . . .

That feral runt on the farm, her belly
swollen. The squeeze of the trigger.
Her shuddering once, not making a sound . . .

The silent, bagged puppies. Their eyes sunken,
as stones in icy pockets of soil shrink
from the cold, hardened surface of the world.

Negative (1996)

The social worker's blond-tipped dreadlocks
are haloed by afternoon light filtering through
the filmy window at 125th and Broadway.

She has pronounced my absolution. But sweating
in relief at this Health Department desk, I think
of everyone I know who's dead or whose lovers

or friends are dead and why do I get to hear
the word that would have saved them. She's talking
still but her words mix and overlap with the ones

in my head. Top. Latex. Bottom. Suck fist carefully
needles water-based. And the letter from Berkeley
in 1983 about a new disease. And jesus, the Quilt

and stepping onto that canvas margin, like wading
ankle-deep into a glassy ocean and being pulled
under by a riptide of sorrow I didn't see coming,

on my hands and knees, like people in the news
who wail and keen over the remains of their brothers,
their husbands, their sons. She's still talking, and I

am thinking of randomness, how if getting fucked
had felt better the first time in '77 or if I'd moved
to San Francisco after school in '82, someone

would be kneeling by my name. The social worker's
condom lecture is a benediction, but she's drowned out
by a solemn march in B-flat minor. Friends, lovers,

teachers, women, men: they're decked out
in prom gowns and combat gear. In slow motion,
from the backs of open cars, they smile and wave.

Two

A Blond Woman

dances in a biker bar
       a young mare
              or marionette
stringless
       loose-limbed
              mesmeric
barefoot on the barroom floor
       I hope she has no man
              not that I want to be hers
I only hope she lives without
       a man's weight
              she sways light
in cutoffs
       sheer white blouse off
              the shoulder
long hair straight
       back to '68
              pouring
over and through
       her uplifted
              arms and hands
the band's efforts
       vindicated
              purified
by her body's
       ministrations
              something
at the base
       of my neck
              stretches her direction
but my feet
       planted
              leaden
Help me
       the band sings
              I think I'm falling.

Bass and Guitar

Drunk one night, Ben the bass player, who gets all the girls, told Andrew, who plays guitar and sings gentle harmony—and the band all sees how he looks at Ben but nobody talks—"You can blow me if you want." Ben doesn't like to think about that night. Neither does Andrew. The road gets long, the bus too narrow, and when Ben brushes past, it sends a twang up Andrew's arm, into his neck and face, desire buzzing against regret like steel strings in sympathetic vibration. He thinks he'd be better if Ben—on his back on the hotel bed—hadn't sighed and touched his face with his fingertips, hadn't tried to stop him at the end, hadn't yanked him from the floor after and kissed him hard on the mouth. But curtains fell as fast behind Ben's face, and Andrew, blindsided, with two pangs, chest and groin, stared then shook his head at poor Ben, let himself out, and padded past door after door to his room at the far end of the glaring hallway. He hates himself for this (he knew better) and hates Ben, a little. But he loves Villa-Lobos, and when he practices on the bus, he wonders that mere nylon, extruded and stretched to breaking over a wooden box, can make such tender, plaintive song.

Mountain Air

In a Village café you spill sugar
On a black tabletop and I remember
Stars in the West Virginia heavens.
Thanksgiving, and my older cousin
And I walked back of the hill.
He'd been playing his guitar. Sheep bells
Reverberated up the steep pastures
Into the night. Shivering in a chair
At the foot of his bed, was I cold? I said no,
And I wasn't: my body was giving me away,
Vibrating from the effort of concealment.
It's been a long time since anything did that.
Until tonight, just now, just before
The words *Come home with me*, murmured
Over this table, planted like seeds.
Notes from my cousin's guitar hang,
Sweet, for a minute, in the still night air.

Across the Galaxy

There was the college room of it:
a fishnet on the walls and ceiling
above a single bed. A turntable on
bookshelves of stacked cinderblock
and pine plank. There was macramé.

There was this boy and that boy,
the night of not-knowing then
knowing. Its bright orange flash.
Two months: nearby towns,
borrowed cars, Greyhounds.

Until a Trailways, and this boy
putting that boy on the last bus out
and all day in his room a singer
on an LP crying for company
and this boy hugging his knees.

Years go by. A house in the hills,
miles of summer. And the singer
on CD: *I'll never have this chance again
No, not like you.* And there was this boy
who, in some ways, never did.

37th Spring

Barefoot in the snow goes the one
who would serve love.

                    —*Camões*

Naked at the window. Morning after
our first night. Dark skin, light. The start of spring,
though snow has dressed the fire escape in stripes,
now softening in the too-high sun: he's late.
Fast kisses, clothes, he dashed without his pack—
books and notes, charts he couldn't do without.
I jumped into jeans, ran after and out
onto the slushed sidewalk: shoeless, unzipped,
tugging my t-shirt down, calling his name.
More breathless kisses. He pulled away, ran
to the corner, slid out of sight. Ten years
sloughed off, and the snow melted at my feet.

Pond

Cicadas in the trees, shrieking Heat! since morning,
have cross-faded to crickets. Frogs and toads add

to the din, more urgent with the pond's darkening.
He's twenty and shucks his cutoffs. I'm sixteen

and not so sure. Then both our clothes lie puddled
in dew-wet grass. To be naked out-of-doors.

He sprints off the dock and I follow, the moon
cresting pines across the pond. Over and over

we plunge through silver into the black water.
We wrench our feet from edge muck, slap mud prints

onto weathered planks with every round. The moon
ascends, the chorus of chirps and thrums resounds

but we go quiet, clinging to a raft, our chins on crossed
forearms, bodies and legs dangling. A giant man-o'-war.

Not-knowing, then knowing: nakedness at night, afloat.
Three miles from the Town of Disapproval, the House

of Wound, the insistent pond licks at our shoulders
and armpits and his fingers on my chest, my stomach

thrilling, my jaw vibrating in discovery. Our limbs entwine
like eels, one hand each daring as far as its reach, until

I let go and slide down his torso, luminous in the teeming
water. A new world, silent but for the pounding in my ears.

Until I have to breathe. He laughs at my zeal, I in relief,
and we kiss. On our lips, the pond, the generous moon.

Morning, Delft Haven

Is it that you've missed
 breakfast or is his sleeping
  skin the color and scent
of coffee and cinnamon?
 Long dancer arms and legs
  and you think of taking a swim
but can't imagine moving
 your head from the small
  of his back. Where you lie,
through the gable window
 sky sea sand blur
  to bands of color—
a Rothko on its side.
 Later a swath of gulls
  in the periwinkle twilight
oddly silent. You will need
 his confirmation—
  Yes. I saw it too.

Last Day, Land's End

Our room at the inn snug as a ship's berth,
windows sealed against late December squalls.
We crawled and slid on each other all day
to get in and out of the corner bed.
That night, a hushed stroll. Up ahead, the mist
teeming within a streetlamp's cone of light.
Coat-to-coat we walked the town, our province;
shops spilled gold squares on the silver pavement.
Dinner brought a swift, sickening panic:
this weekend on the Cape was all we'd get.
I didn't let on. While we ambled back
my dread dissolved into the kissing fog,
too dense for us to see the lighthouse sweep
the bay, though we could hear its soulful tone.

Night-for-Night

Scene: a downpour. Bicycle, coastal town.
Streetlamps. Rider's shirt is soaked to the skin.
Heedless, he stops at a familiar lawn.
Tight close-up: he's watching them like a film.
After their first sex scene, with lidded eyes
one whispered he likes to watch "the movies."
Stay here, thought the other, but when he tried
he saw, even smelled, a stand of fir trees.
One will leave the other for the desert,
thirty mythic acres near Santa Fe.
The sun, obscured by sky-blue clouds at first,
will slip out, waver, slide into the bay.
 Seven years on, this midnight *mise en scène*:
 a bike, a lawn, relentless summer rain.

There's a Bar in Florence

called Crisco Club. Three domains, progressively dimmer: cocktails, porno lounge, "dark room." I've got a pocket guide and twenty words. One is *negroni*: equal parts gin, Campari, sweet vermouth. The bartender squeezes a slice of blood orange in approval. The lounge disappoints (California porn) and I retreat from Three—*too* dark. Back at the bar, in walks Danger. Shaved head, green eyes, chiseled under an open shirt. He cracks a smile and my barstool tilts. Then he's gone. If he's not in the lounge, *I'm going in.* All dusty day I imagined an evening. Open-air café, bottle of wine. Lace curtains in an easy breeze and two dappled forms on white sheets. But—Somewhere a dull red bulb. Shapes emerging from black, like images in a developer bath. I spot him watching two others and approach, oblique, as if toward them. At the last minute, I veer thirty degrees and the two of us fall against a wall, *appassionato.* I want to leave with him, can only muster "May I see you in the light" which makes him laugh. We stay, vertical, air hot and unmoving as a boiler room's. I want to see him in the light. His mouth is a feast. Helpless, I finish. His hands and lips on an interloper before I can even wipe off and button up. I stumble onto the street at midnight, swabbing my forehead with a napkin. Past the Duomo tarted up in artificial light, I start across the cobblestones to my narrow room at the *penzione.* But—In the portico, coming toward me. Blond hair to his shoulders. Three tongues between us: chipped Spanish, English, Italian. Adriano, student of architecture. We jump the low wall of an ancient bridge and sit facing the Ponte Vecchio, shoulders pressed. He takes my hand. A long walk on the far side of the river. We climb stone stairs to a high piazza (the Michelangelo) and look back over the city. Quiet, glowing. On the way down, he stops under a tree, lamplight dappling his sculpted face. Adriano lies back in the gentle grass. My train in four hours. We take our time. Someone always leaves.

Village of Adiós

Overarching palms with scissor edges clack
   and lacerate the seldom breeze. Geckos
stick to walls, they bob and click.

   I tick off ten times ten steps
from the white hotel down to the water's edge:
   Playa la Ropa, beach of upwashed clothes.

Naked under a striped robe from another
   hemisphere, I pale here. I've come
alone to find what we may have lost.

   What I discover is tender
octopus in garlic, sparkle of cold cerveza
   por favor. At night a bar, a beach.

Rainy season but the rains don't come.
   Sweat down my back, tequila
and tiritas—slivered fish bathed in lime.

   Yesterday, a diving mask,
another bay, facedown on the taut
   membrane between what I knew

and this other all-but-silent world of glint
   and hover, flash and dart yellow silver
blue and I couldn't breathe.

   At week's end, I leave the hushed vowels
of the couple next door for the consonant surf
   a hundred feet below. Waves in breaths

against the sand. Under gathering clouds,
       I wade chest-deep in the warm blue bay.
When cold droplets tap my skin, I listen.

       And they sound like the goodbye I dread
and long for. Rain filling cupped palms,
       cooling my upturned face.

Three

Opening

I'd arrive in time for two
glasses, the first drunk
quickly, the second for
something in the hand.

There'd be a tongue on a wall,
and a mustached Buddha
from telephone books. I
would be not looking for you.

I'd find you scrutinizing
a microscopic slide through
a magnifying lens. I'd sidle:
What do you think? You'd say

We should try again, without
looking up, without a flinch.
I'd come back with *I meant
the miniatures.* You: *Yes. I like them.*

And facing me now *I'd like
to try again.* I might say *All right*,
and we'd return to the ashen
wasteland, exquisite in its rendering.

Bathtub Ophelia

on viewing an untitled color photo from
Ellen M. Blalock's series, "A New Rite"

slipped from supple arms
cracked her heart

like a brown egg
on the ungiving rim

a mere skim of white
porcelain on iron

what issue this
blood red wisp

from blood red slip
knees gripped as if

she could save
herself still

Vietnam

In the birthday photo, my smiling aunt
has her back to the wide-open window,
behind her the unseen Albemarle night.
Summer '68 must have been abuzz.
After chicken and dishes, we'd have swayed
on the porch till maybe dark. Lightning bugs
would be shooting their tiny flares. We'd wait
to hear the whippoorwill's tattoo before
reassembling for cake and striped ice cream.
In the darkened living room, a ghost dot
on the TV screen, cooling from the news.
That afternoon, I'd have tossed the severed
heads to Rex, examined the violet
gizzards, helped pluck the scalded remains.

Unspoken at JFK

Laptop battery sapped, finally a corner of floor
by a free outlet. Soon, a muscled man with a buzz-cut
and the same need. Stateside on leave, this sergeant
was headed back to Baghdad, no questions asked,

and did I want to see some photos. Before and after
shots: rows of tents where there'd been only sand. *See how
much better*, he said. *No*, I thought, but what I said was
I was Army, too—captain, before I could weigh that word.

The slightest nod. He didn't ask where or when, I didn't offer.
I didn't tell him about the weekend, the rally, the march
against the war. *How about more photos*, some he didn't show
most people. My stomach gripped. Before I could answer,

he started pulling up folders on his desktop, my pulse racing
with the first double-click. He took them from the back
of a HUM-V he said, while the hourglass icon hovered
like a hypnotist's pocket watch. Before I could run,

the first photo bled across the screen—blues and pink,
lavenders—a sunset. Then dozens. Clouds limned in silver.
This red-faced career soldier about my age, back to Baghdad
no question: smitten with pastels and shimmer, the quality of light.

Testament (To My Sister)

You leave the service with me in a jar.
How old will you be by then? Past eighty:
still a blonde, I bet. And still a beauty.
Your children (middle-aged) follow in cars
with partners, kids—but who can see that far?
In seven days you'll gather at the tree,
the ancient hemlock on your property.
I always liked that corner of the yard.
You hand your 40-something son the spade.
He lifts a circle of sod, wipes his eyes.
Your girl, whose ginger hair by now has grayed,
pours my ashes around the tree and tries
in vain to make a joke I might have made.
She and I are lousy at goodbyes.

Well-Worn Hills

for Linda

My friend on her knees
before a white birch sapling.
Front yard of the house
they loved. Now her hands in his
ashes. How she's smoothing him.

The Middle of March

The snow has pulled back
from the house and left a hem
of brown leaves, flattened
and damp as a lover's hair
the moment before she wakes.

I Sang in Her Wedding

In her basement, dodging a mound of laundry, we pass,
close. She radiates, the hairs on my arm raise. Upstairs,
her son, a grownup sixteen. And the man she married

at forty, three children of his own. She wore white linen,
her hair up, which I'd never seen. Two strands kept freeing
themselves. Her son there, ten. She'd left her boyfriend

at thirty, a surprise next month, part of him taken root. Moving
day, an upstairs bedroom, boxes all around, child on the way,
she wondered aloud Could we...? but I hedged. It had been

seven years since that week, that summer. Inside her,
in awe. The pink pearls (velvet case, satin lining)
she kept hidden under her bed, but showed me once

the summer before. Both of us finishing school, mending
from separate heartaches, our lips pressing good night,
longer each night, but we'd agreed only they were ready.

Could we have? Would she have what she needs? Would I?
I'd have a son. The boy with trees in his name she kept
from his father at first, but would have shared with me.

Ecstasy

after Roethke

I have known the exquisite pleasure of hand tools
Strewn about the floor, ecstasy of level and plumbline,
Mirth of mitre saw and measurements,
Elation in sawdust-covered work spaces,
Congenial bathroom, basement, back porch,
Unmitigated rapture of hammer and nail,
Ritual of roller, brush, paint,
Delightful repetition of staple gun and screen.
And I have seen leaves from the branches of trees,
Finer than flower petals, alive, more golden than sunlight,
Drift, almost silent, through long hammock afternoons,
Draping as adornments onto stones and ephemeral ferns,
Dressing the soft grass, the rich moist fertile earth.

A Distant Line of Hills

The air is clear, and leaves, undone,
drift in zigzags—russet, crimson.
Wild purple phlox and goldenrod
in rearview mirrors wave and nod,
like summer's parting guests. And on

the complicated road we run
we take a deeper breath. The sun
ignites a sumac's velvet pods.
       The air is clear

and apple-crisp; light is honey
on tree trunks in the afternoon.
We didn't know, and find that odd:
behind the slowly molting woods
lies a long and low horizon.
       The air is clear.

Winter Hike

A narrow packed trail, drifts two feet deep on either side,
will remain weeks past the spring thaw, a spine along
the mountain's back, meandering reminder. In a bottom,
a pool topped with gray-green ice the color of your eyes.

Brook gurgling, unseen beneath fine lines in a sheer
translucent layer. You knew the way but I knew the trees:
the beeches' smooth gray trunks, their rows of shivering
leaves like paper sparrows. White pine, and another kind.

On the barren rise, all stone and glare and New York City
improbable in the distance. Ahead, hemlock shadows
feathered across the snow, ours moving among them.
An impossible blue sky, a first kiss. And the glisten.

Crossing

Late the night my grandmother died, I dreamed
I walked beneath a pillowed sky alone
through wheat fields quilted white, the fences seams.
I headed for the woods instead of home.
The cold, the light, the late November snow
made ground and sky so bright they hurt my eyes.
Or was it something lost, I didn't know,
but in the dream I cried, or tried to cry.
I knew I'd never make it to the woods—
I had to catch a boat back to a feast.
Many strangers. Tables laden with food.
I leaned from door to door but didn't eat.
    When I awoke, her absence was a wound
    that bloomed inside my chest, and filled the room.

Near Mercy Park

He sees the "other" woman now and then
and goes for long walks with his aged dog,
sometimes jogs when his knee is up to it.
He rambles, putters in the big cold house,
reads about history, airplanes, and war.
Sometimes late at night he wakens, enraged,
and can't believe what's happened to his life.
He screams and shakes his head, and even cries.

The old man who rarely fed his daughter
or his son, and never once the grandkids,
found a pair of kittens under the porch.
The brother gallops about, bucks and rears.
The sister's front paws are badly malformed,
so he has to hold and feed her by hand.

Raptor

On my hands and knees in the woods
below the house, I'm rummaging,
looking to introduce the wild shrub
I've pilfered from the grove down the hill.
There, where the brook meets the wider creek,
the rhododendron are taller than I am,
bare trunks thick as an arm, oval leaves
spread like hands in the understory.

I have never felt more alone. But soon I sense
and stand to face at twenty feet and bearing down:
talons, beak, and wings four feet across.
At ten feet, no more, the startled bird pulls up
and perches. Red-tailed hawk. We regard
each other for minutes—I the more astounded.
With a slight contraction, the hawk
pushes off and glides downhill, noiseless.

On all fours on the rich forest floor, I've returned
to roots and rock, clearing a nook of last fall
and (underneath) the fall before, each layer
more earth, less leaf, than the last. I reason
that worrying the dry leaves must have sounded
from a height like nesting, scurry. But hawks
hunt open fields. Their eyes and ears are keen.
How to explain—this: *We are never alone.*

You Said Listen

It was one of those songs—
shut us up at the turnoff,
kept us in the truck
that night, our dashboard
eyes on the radio dial—
Could you see it like me . . . .

Now I see you hated it
here in the hills
unnerved by the night
but you never let on
and that—finally—
is a kind of love.

Say You're Walking on a Beach

and it's twilight, the brilliant day having begun its fade to indigo. The water is passive, expectant, more lake than sea. Suppose there's a small boat a few feet offshore, and it slides onto the sand. You approach, and place your hands on its weathered prow, wood thickened with layers of paint, dark green and white. The boat is empty—no oars or engine. If you hoist yourself into the hull, wide enough your arms just reach one side to the other, a wave might lift and draw the boat into the water. And what if by now there's a canopy of stars; if the tide, sky, and sinuous line of hills in the distance—they feel like comfort—are all shades of the same deep blue? Thin clouds focus the moonlight into five silvery beams, yet the stars are bright enough to be doubled in the generous sea. Say the boat rocks a little, drifting, then realigns and starts to follow the shore. And if it's moving backward, flat stern first? You'd want to turn, wouldn't you, to see what's ahead, behind you. But suppose you didn't. If instead, you lay back and took in the stars, the sea's sweet breeze on your skin. Could you do this? Is it enough to know you are in the boat?

Last Will

When a box of ash is all that's left,
don't revere me on a mantelpiece
or let me get enshrined on a shelf.
Spill me in a wave, a salty breeze.
Better yet, just turn me in the heap
behind the house with other compost,
rotted leaf remains, trimmings you keep
stockpiling, so nothing's ever lost.
Trouble me in this darkening stew—
coffee grounds, potato peels, earthworms—
rich and moist the further down you go,
and notice: at the bottom, warmer.
Dishevel me in autumn. Come June,
look for me in every iris bloom.

If We Went Back to Maple Ridge

The long dirt drive to the white frame house
will have gone green from lack of wear
except for twin tracks too hard-packed

for even the hardiest weed. The border
of forsythia, though a massive tangle, still
a hallelujah chorus in the spring.

Amid the heavy-scented lilies, they lined up
to view our grandmother. My sister and I,
in our thirties, stood at the back wall of the parlor.

The front edge of the yard defined by daffodils,
but harder to divine now between lawn and lane.
The house diminished between taller trees,

the roof begun to sag along its spine,
rust in patches on the silvered tin,
like the Indian Pony we rode past its prime.

We didn't go up to look. We knew—
the coif, cheeks too pink, the lid's tufted satin.
Not everything must be seen to be remembered.

The swingless porch littered by how many autumns,
and flat slates leading around back now snaggle-toothed
and tombstoned by frost heave, the oaks' gnarled roots.

Hefty nephews, our distant cousins, had been assigned
to lift the coffin, but we replaced two of the six and, one
on each end, bore her out and into the hearse's long maw.

We won't go back to the farm. Her gardens are no doubt
overrun with pokeweed, johnson grass, a few prickly cedars.
The sheds must list and crack like ships caught in the Arctic.

But in hottest summer, jar flies—what she called cicadas—
still punctuate the day. The whippoorwill announces
every evening, the cadence of crickets and katydids all night.

Epilogue: As New York Snow

By two o'clock the snowstorm had begun
its diagonal attack on windows
overlooking East 7th. Inside, low
hum of the fridge. Hard to tell when the sun
went down: the night sky retained a special
glower: crystals, infinitesimal
mirrors, falling, reflect who we are. Sky
the color of burn. Nothing here is pure.

But in the morning upper branches lace
themselves in a graceful matrix. Ivy
firmly woven onto the fire escape
shivers a little less in the rising
slant of the sun. This day will be clean. Let
us meet in the sober and snowswept light.

Notes

"Snake Hunting": The last line is a colloquialism, a contraction of "indeed," spoken for emphasis by my great aunts (and others) from Franklin, West Virginia.

The photographs referenced in "Odalisque '76" and "Bathtub Ophelia" are in the permanent collection at Light Work on the campus of Syracuse University.

"A Blond Woman": italicized line from "Help Me," Joni Mitchell. *Court and Spark*. Asylum, 1974.

"Across the Galaxy": title and italicized line from "Company," Rickie Lee Jones. *Rickie Lee Jones*. Warner Bros., 1979.

"Night-for-Night": In cinematography, night-for-night filming is the practice of filming night scenes at night, as opposed to the older practice of filming during the day, and later "correcting" the film via a variety of post-production techniques.

"Opening" was prompted by a visit to a gallery featuring the work of Marion Wilson.

"Vietnam": Albemarle County is located in Central Virginia.

"You Said Listen": italicized line from "Because I Told You So," Jonatha Brooke. Recorded by Mary Ann Redmond. *Here I Am*. Spellbound Music, 2000.

About the Author

David Eye earned an MFA in Creative Writing from Syracuse University in 2008, and his poetry and prose have since appeared in a variety of journals and anthologies. David has received scholarships to the 2014 Sewanee Writers' Conference and the 2016 West Chester University Poetry Conference; he is the winner of the 2014 Hudson Valley Writers Guild Non-Fiction Award in humor; and he was a finalist in the 2015-2016 Tennessee Williams Poetry Contest, selected by Yusef Komunyakaa. David has taught creative writing, academic writing, and literature at Syracuse University, St. John's University, Manhattan College, and Cazenovia College. Before he turned to writing, David enjoyed a seventeen-year career as an actor/singer in New York, regional theatres, and national tours. Before moving to New York, David spent four years in the military, stationed at Fort Sam Houston in San Antonio, Texas. He grew up in rural Virginia, and lives (for now) at the edge of a forest in the Catskill Mountains.

About the Artist

Parnell Corder is an award-winning botanical illustrator. Originally from Indianapolis, he studied at the School of the Art Institute of Chicago and lives in Los Angeles.

THE HILARY THAM CAPITAL COLLECTION

Nathalie F. Anderson, *Stain*

Mel Belin, *Flesh That Was Chrysalis*

Carrie Bennett, *The Land Is a Painted Thing*

Doris Brody, *Judging the Distance*

Sarah Browning, *Whiskey in the Garden of Eden*

Grace Cavalieri, *Pinecrest Rest Haven*

Cheryl Clarke, *By My Precise Haircut*

Christopher Conlon, *Gilbert and Garbo in Love*
       & *Mary Falls: Requiem for Mrs. Surratt*

Donna Denizé, *Broken like Job*

W. Perry Epes, *Nothing Happened*

David Eye, *Seed*

Bernadette Geyer, *The Scabbard of Her Throat*

Barbara G. S. Hagerty, *Twinzilla*

James Hopkins, *Eight Pale Women*

Brandon Johnson, *Love's Skin*

Marilyn McCabe, *Perpetual Motion*

Judith McCombs, *The Habit of Fire*

James McEwen, *Snake Country*

Miles David Moore, *The Bears of Paris*
       & *Rollercoaster*

Kathi Morrison-Taylor, *By the Nest*

Tera Vale Ragan, *Reading the Ground*

Michael Shaffner, *The Good Opinion of Squirrels*

Maria Terrone, *The Bodies We Were Loaned*

Hilary Tham, *Bad Names for Women*
       & *Counting*

Barbara Louise Ungar, *Charlotte Brontë, You Ruined My Life*
       & *Immortal Medusa*

Jonathan Vaile, *Blue Cowboy*

Rosemary Winslow, *Green Bodies*

Michele Wolf, *Immersion*

Joe Zealberg, *Covalence*

OTHER WORD WORKS BOOKS

Annik Adey-Babinski, *Okay Cool No Smoking Love Pony*
Karren L. Alenier, *Wandering on the Outside*
Karren L. Alenier, ed., *Whose Woods These Are*
Karren L. Alenier & Miles David Moore, eds.,
      Winners: A Retrospective of the Washington Prize
Christopher Bursk, ed., *Cool Fire*
Barbara Goldberg, *Berta Broadfoot and Pepin the Short*
Frannie Lindsay, *If Mercy*
Elaine Magarrell, *The Madness of Chefs*
Marilyn McCabe, *Glass Factory*
Ann Pelletier, *Letter That Never*
Ayaz Pirani, *Happy You Are Here*
W.T. Pfefferle, *My Coolest Shirt*
Jacklyn Potter, Dwaine Rieves, Gary Stein, eds.,
      Cabin Fever: Poets at Joaquin Miller's Cabin
Robert Sargent, *Aspects of a Southern Story*
      & *A Woman from Memphis*
Fritz Ward, *Tsunami Diorama*
Amber West, *Hen & God*
Nancy White, ed., *Word for Word*

THE TENTH GATE PRIZE

Jennifer Barber, *Works on Paper*, 2015
Roger Sedarat, *Haji as Puppet*, 2016
Lisa Sewell, *Impossible Object*, 2014

THE WASHINGTON PRIZE

Nathalie F. Anderson, *Following Fred Astaire*, 1998

Michael Atkinson, *One Hundred Children Waiting for a Train*, 2001

Molly Bashaw, *The Whole Field Still Moving Inside It*, 2013

Carrie Bennett, *biography of water*, 2004

Peter Blair, *Last Heat*, 1999

John Bradley, *Love-in-Idleness: The Poetry of Roberto Zingarello*, 1995, 2nd edition 2014

Christopher Bursk, *The Way Water Rubs Stone*, 1988

Richard Carr, *Ace*, 2008

Jamison Crabtree, *Rel[AM]ent*, 2014

Jessica Cuello, *Hunt*, 2016

B. K. Fischer, *St. Rage's Vault*, 2012

Linda Lee Harper, *Toward Desire*, 1995

Ann Rae Jonas, *A Diamond Is Hard But Not Tough*, 1997

Frannie Lindsay, *Mayweed*, 2009

Richard Lyons, *Fleur Carnivore*, 2005

Elaine Magarrell, *Blameless Lives*, 1991

Fred Marchant, *Tipping Point*, 1993, 2nd edition 2013

Ron Mohring, *Survivable World*, 2003

Barbara Moore, *Farewell to the Body*, 1990

Brad Richard, *Motion Studies*, 2010

Jay Rogoff, *The Cutoff*, 1994

Prartho Sereno, *Call from Paris*, 2007, 2nd edition 2013

Enid Shomer, *Stalking the Florida Panther*, 1987

John Surowiecki, *The Hat City After Men Stopped Wearing Hats*, 2006

Miles Waggener, *Phoenix Suites*, 2002

Charlotte Warren, *Gandhi's Lap*, 2000

Mike White, *How to Make a Bird with Two Hands*, 2011

Nancy White, *Sun, Moon, Salt*, 1992, 2nd edition 2010

George Young, *Spinoza's Mouse*, 1996

INTERNATIONAL EDITIONS

Kajal Ahmad (Alana Marie Levinson-LaBrosse, Mewan
   Nahro Said Sofi, and Darya Abdul-Karim Ali Najin,
   trans., with Barbara Goldberg), *Handful of Salt*
Keyne Cheshire (trans.), *Murder at Jagged Rock: A Tragedy by*
   Sophocles
Jean Cocteau (Mary-Sherman Willis, trans.), *Grace Notes*
Yoko Danno & James C. Hopkins, *The Blue Door*
Moshe Dor, Barbara Goldberg, Giora Leshem, eds.,
   The Stones Remember: Native Israeli Poets
Moshe Dor (Barbara Goldberg, trans.), *Scorched by the Sun*
Lee Sang (Myong-Hee Kim, trans.), *Crow's Eye View:*
   The Infamy of Lee Sang, Korean Poet
Vladimir Levchev (Henry Taylor, trans.), *Black Book of*
   the Endangered Species

CPSIA information can be obtained
at www.ICGtesting.com
Printed in the USA
FFOW05n1427080117

9 781944 585143